This Animal Coloring Book Belongs To...

_____

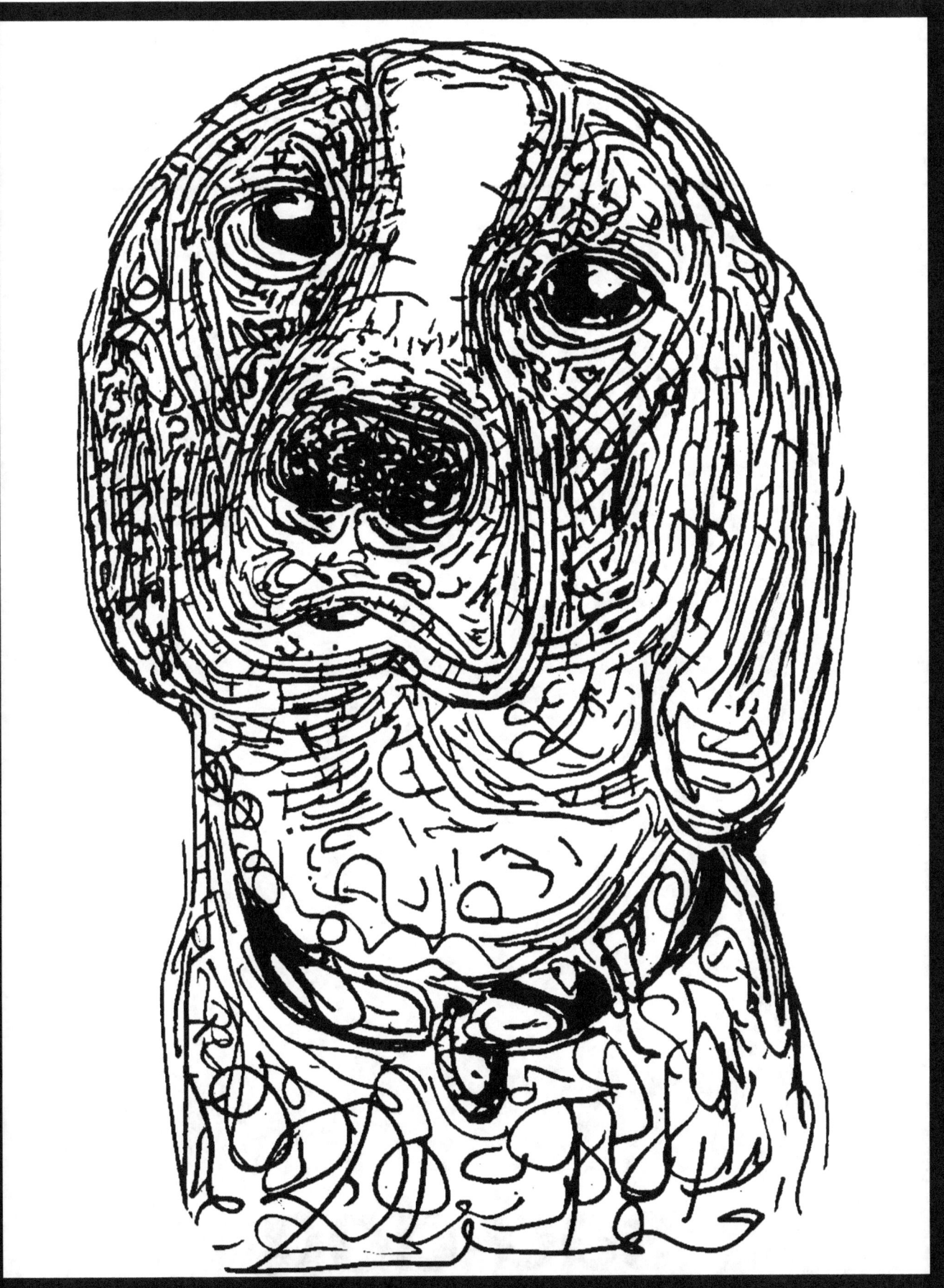

sad dog

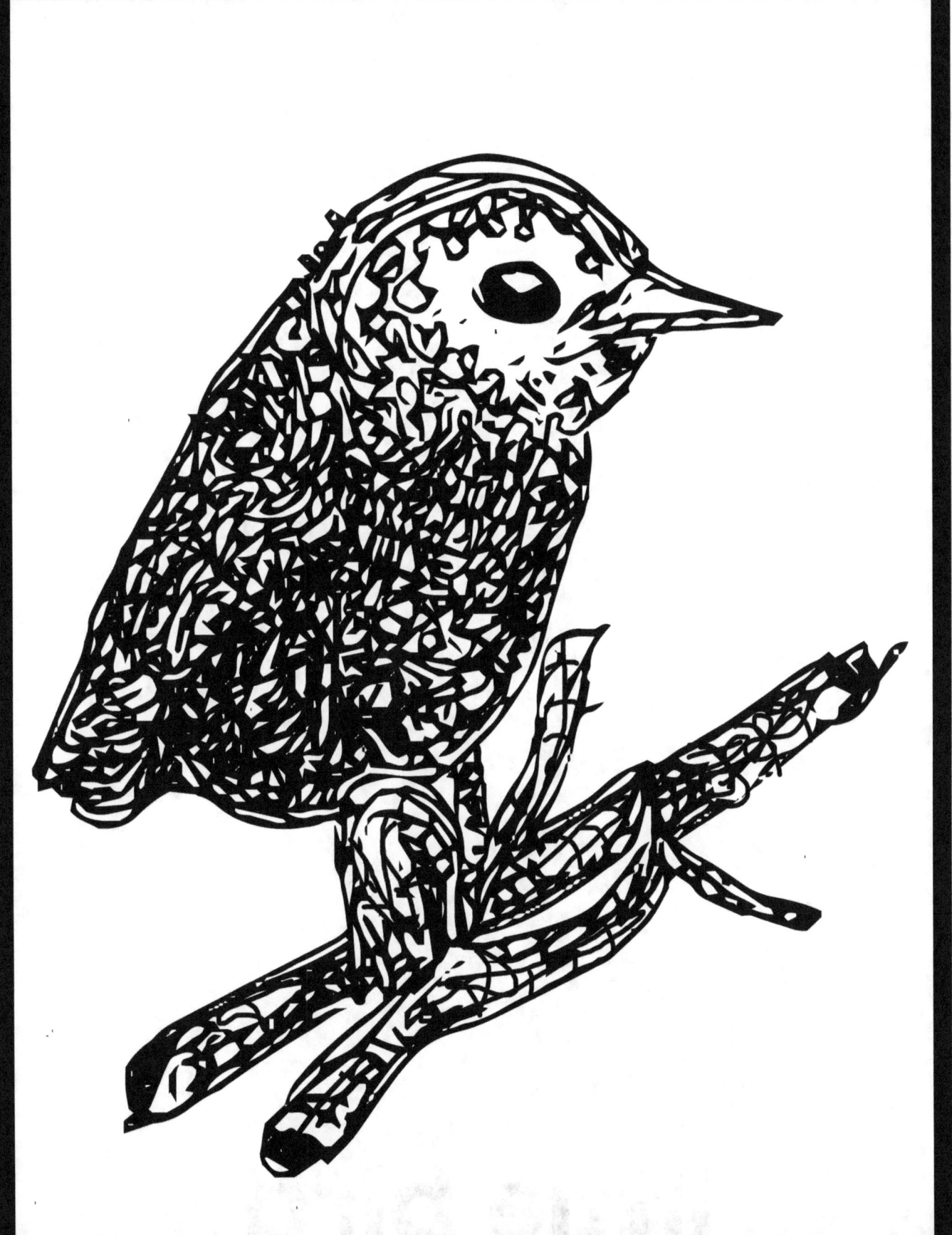

little bird

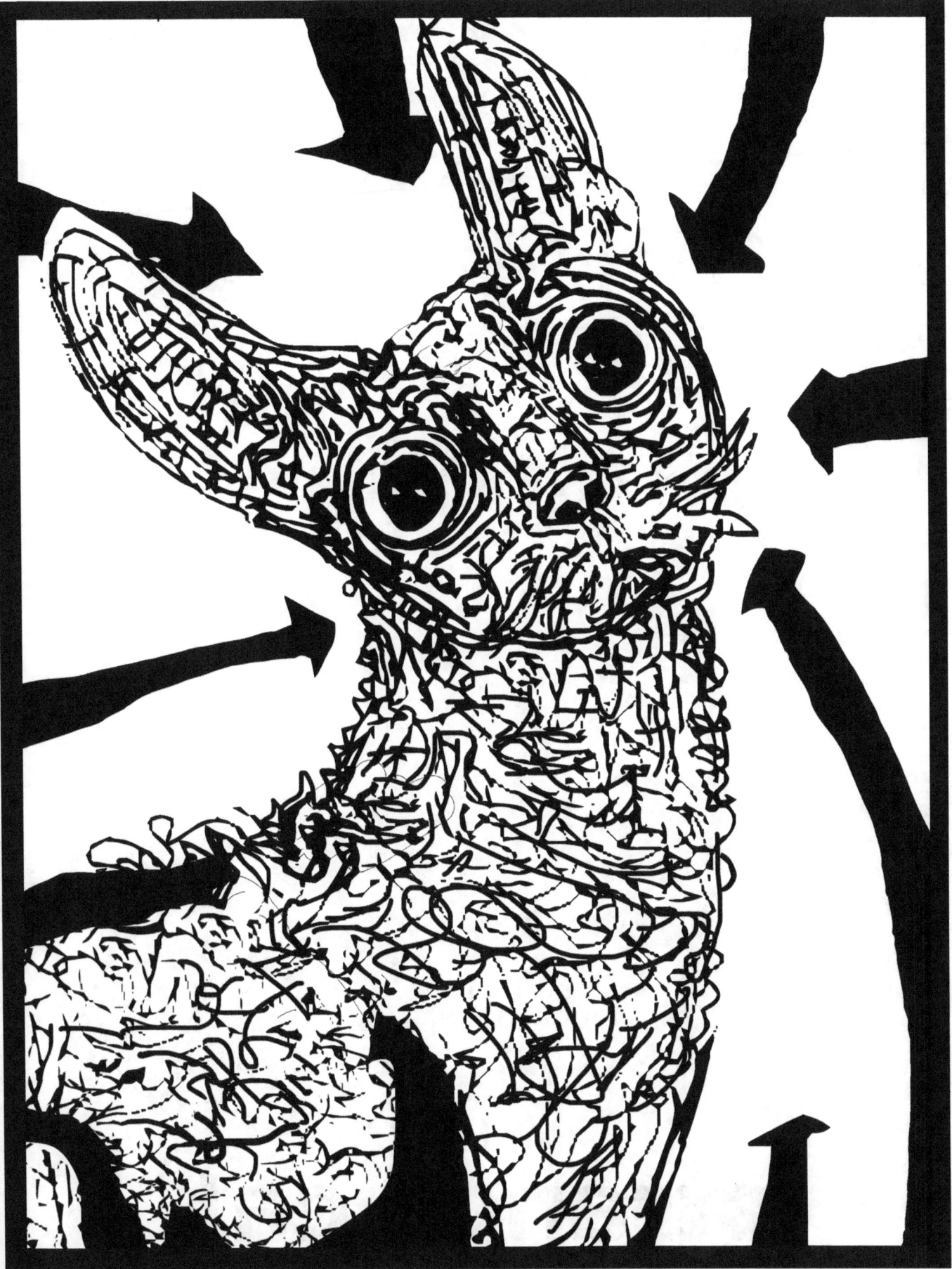

strange cat

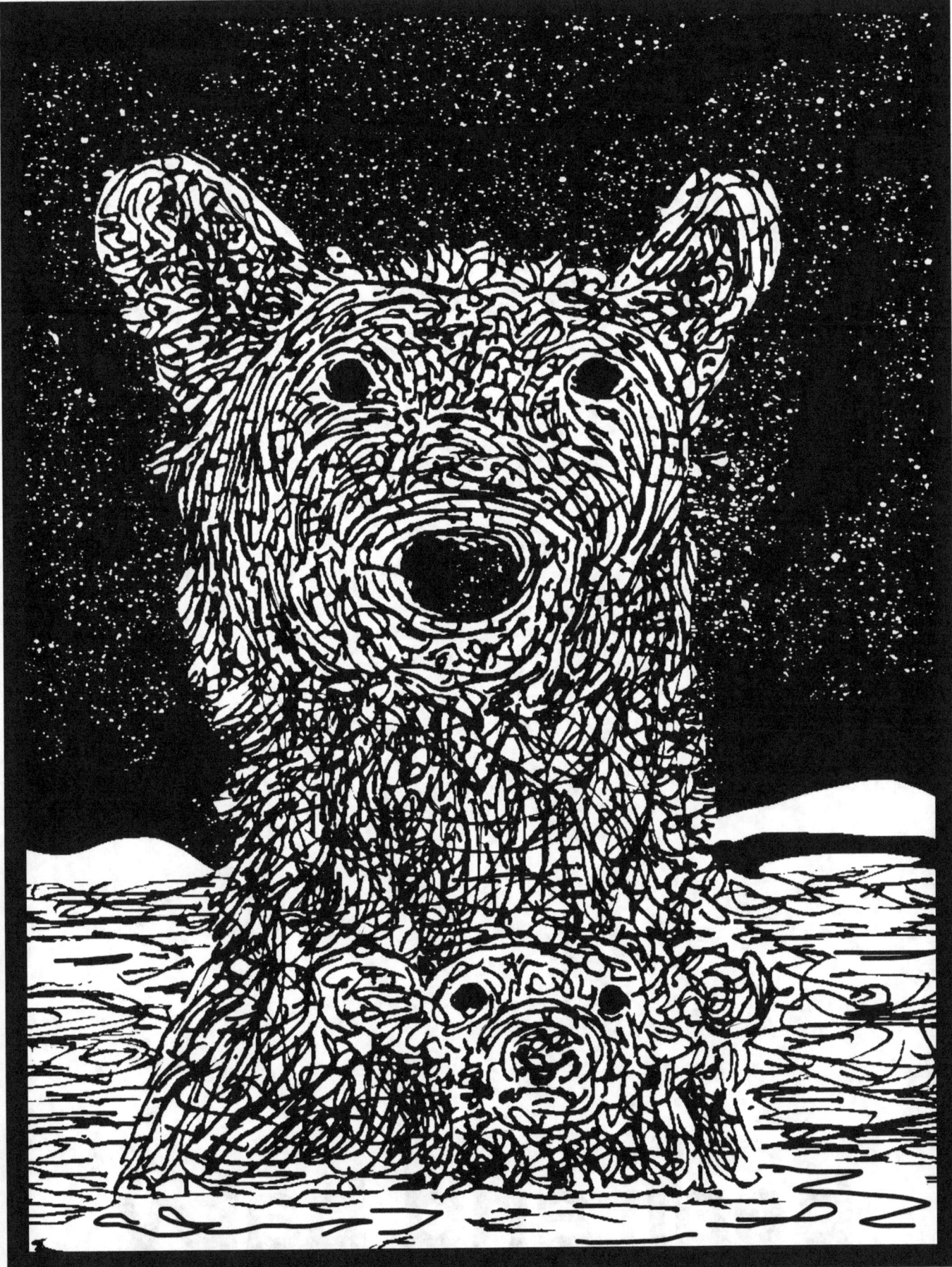

bear and baby

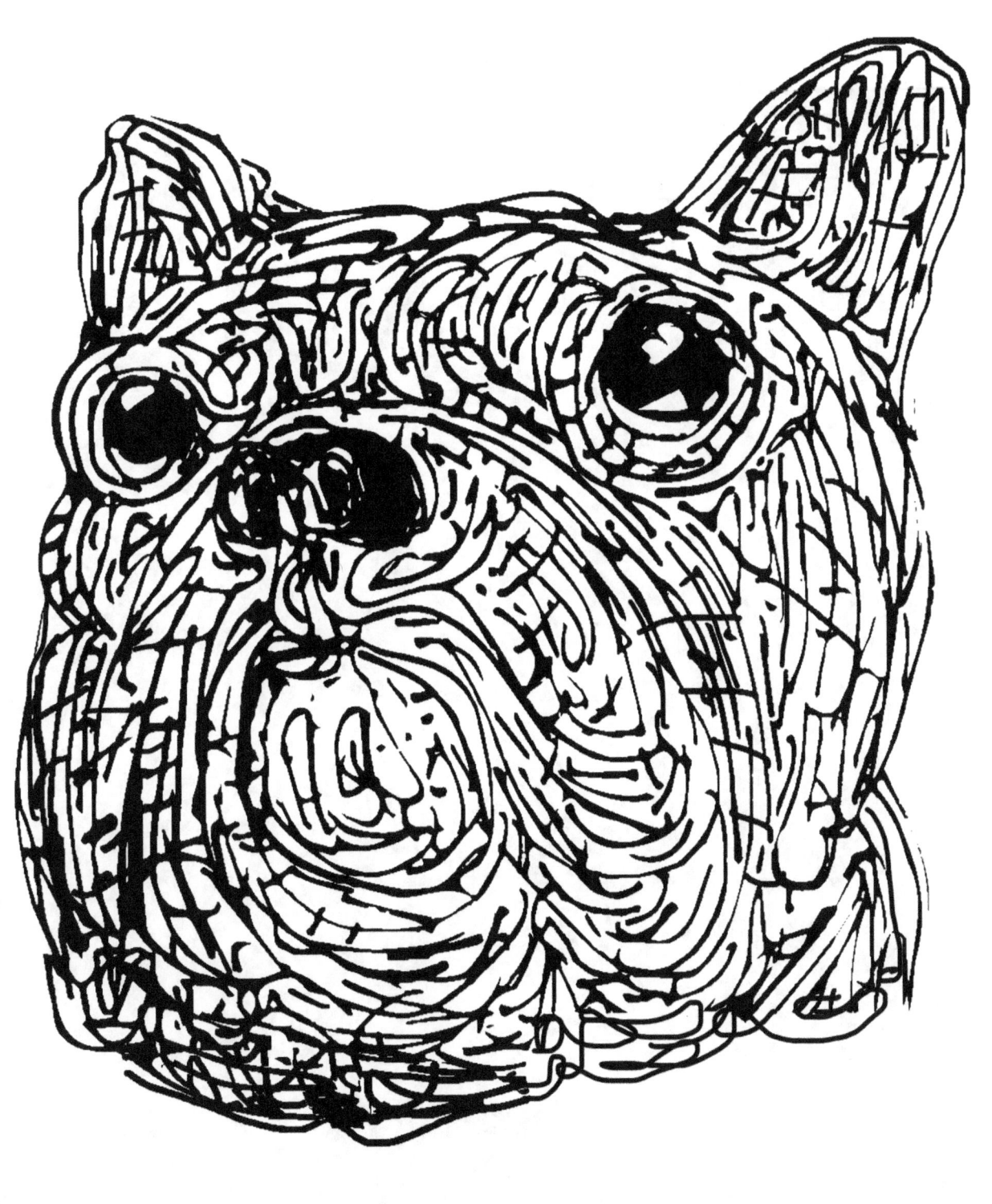

serious dog

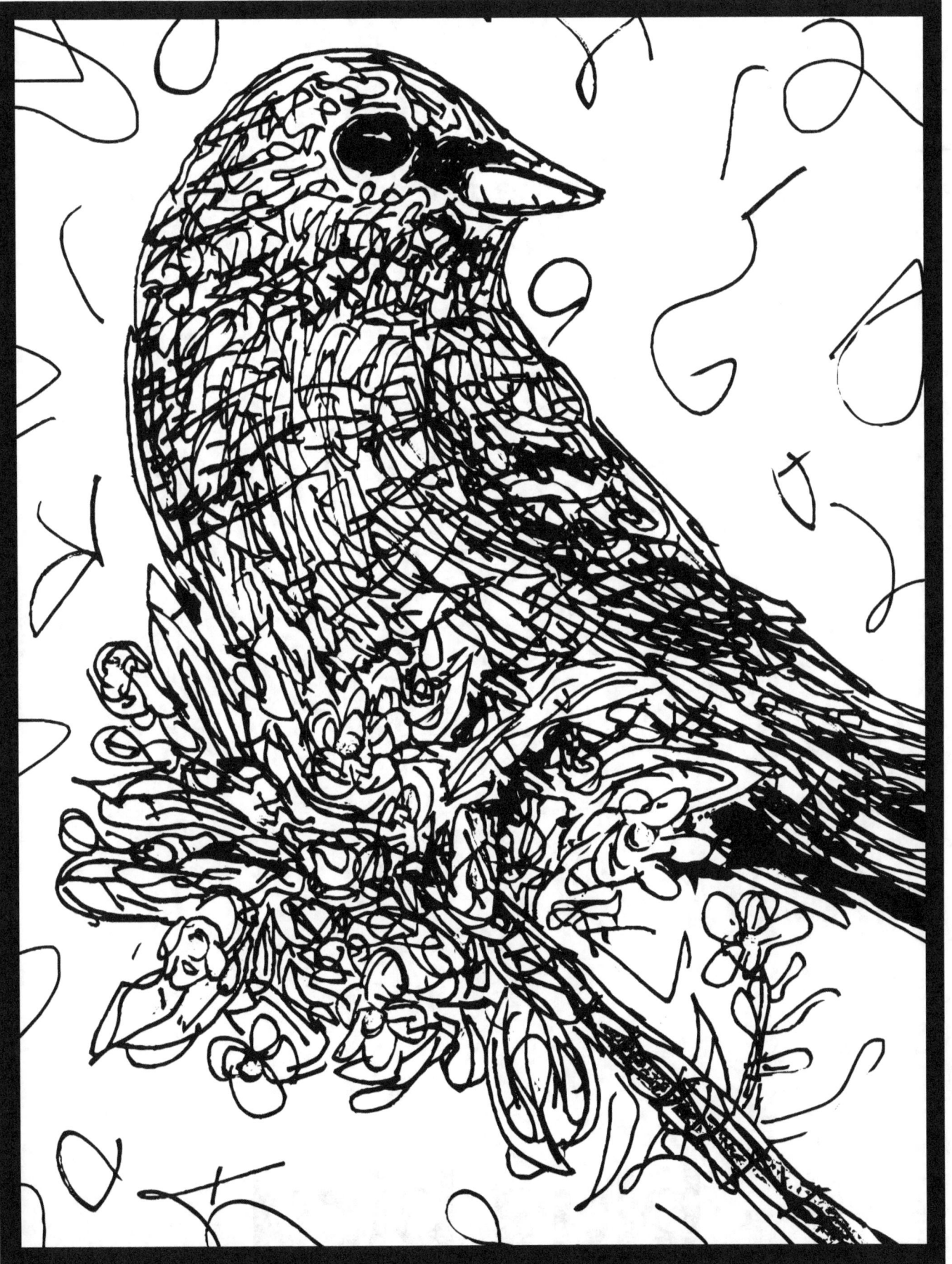

blue bird

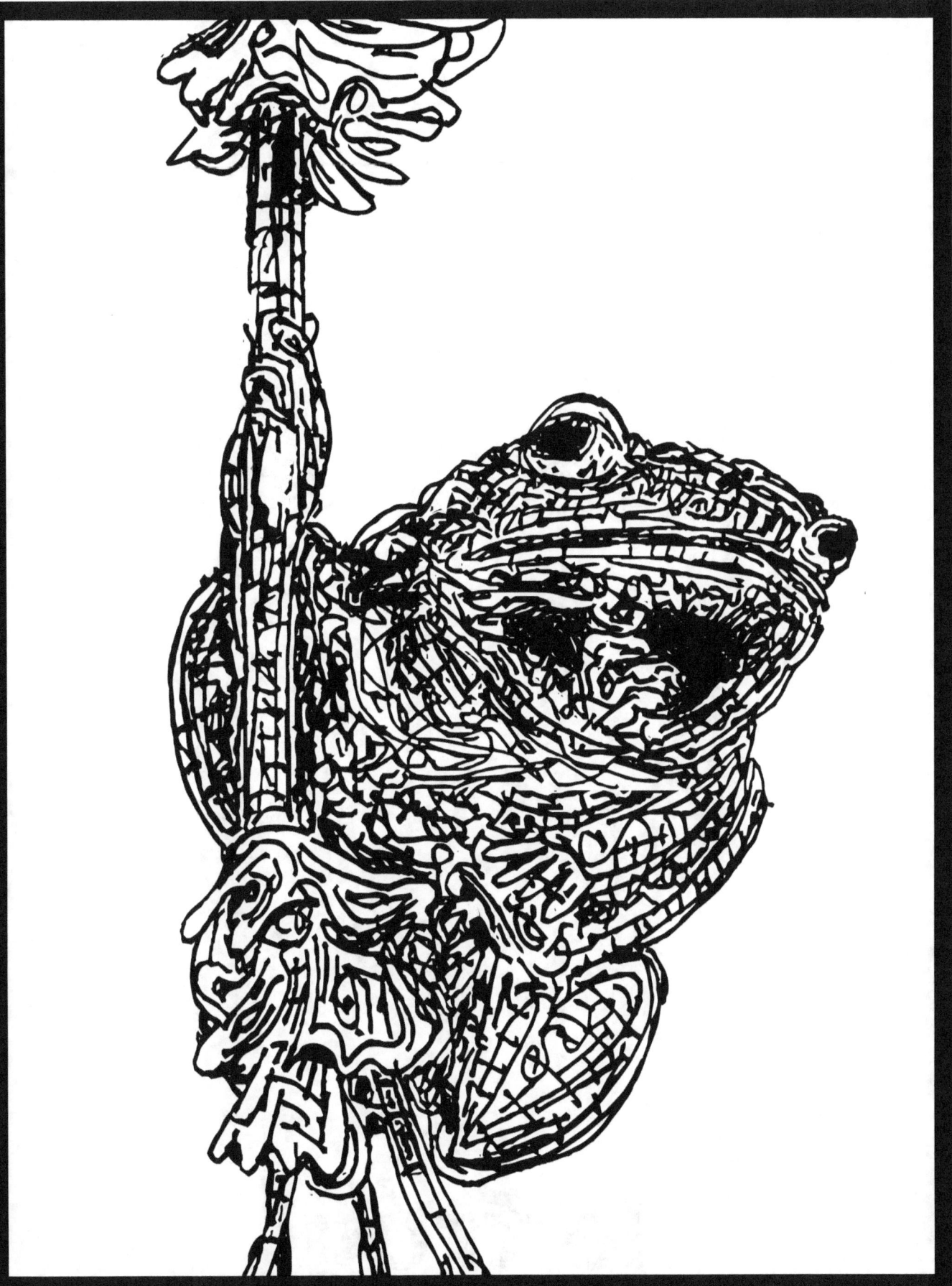

le frog

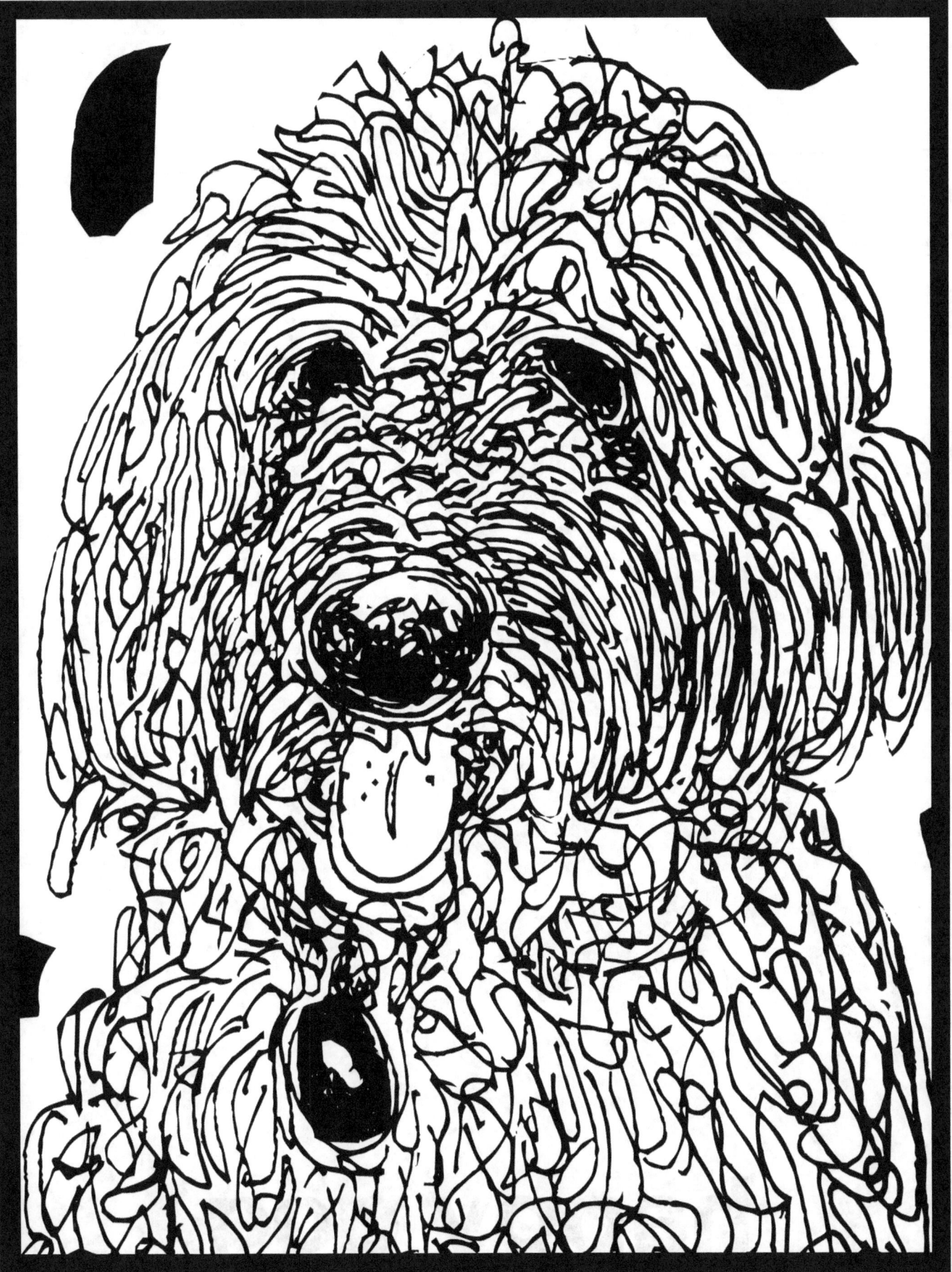

happy dog

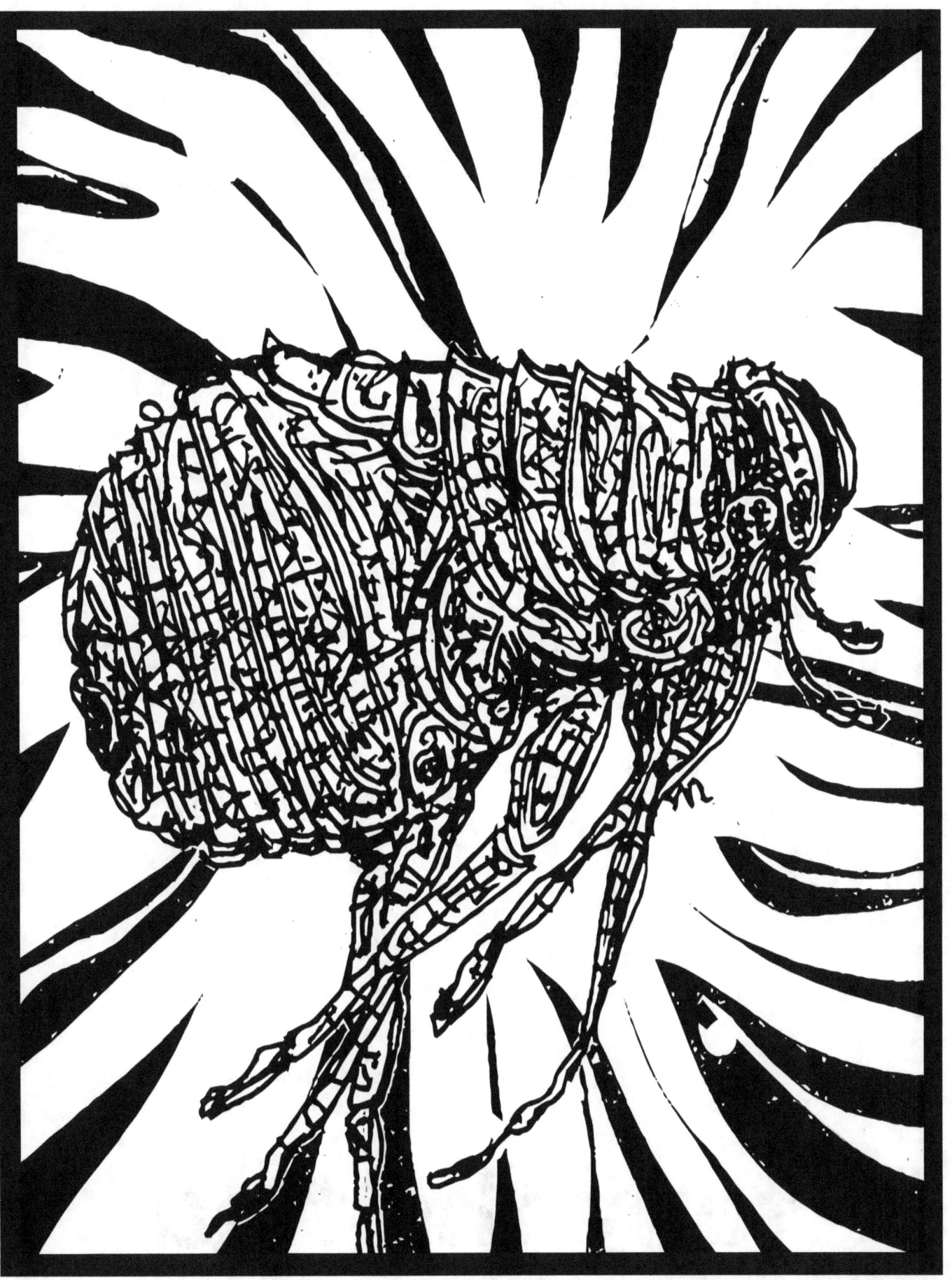

tony the flea

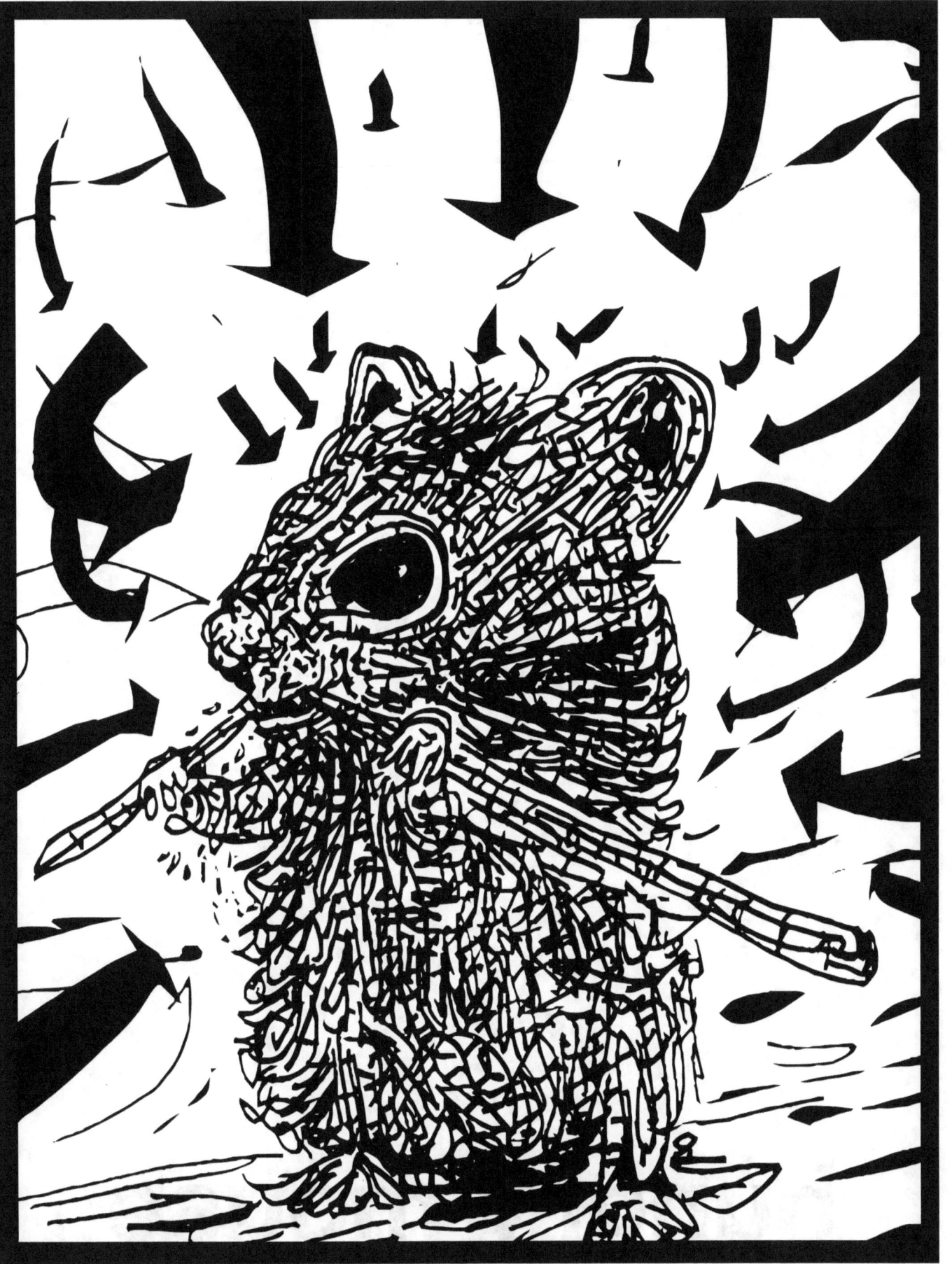

hungry mouse

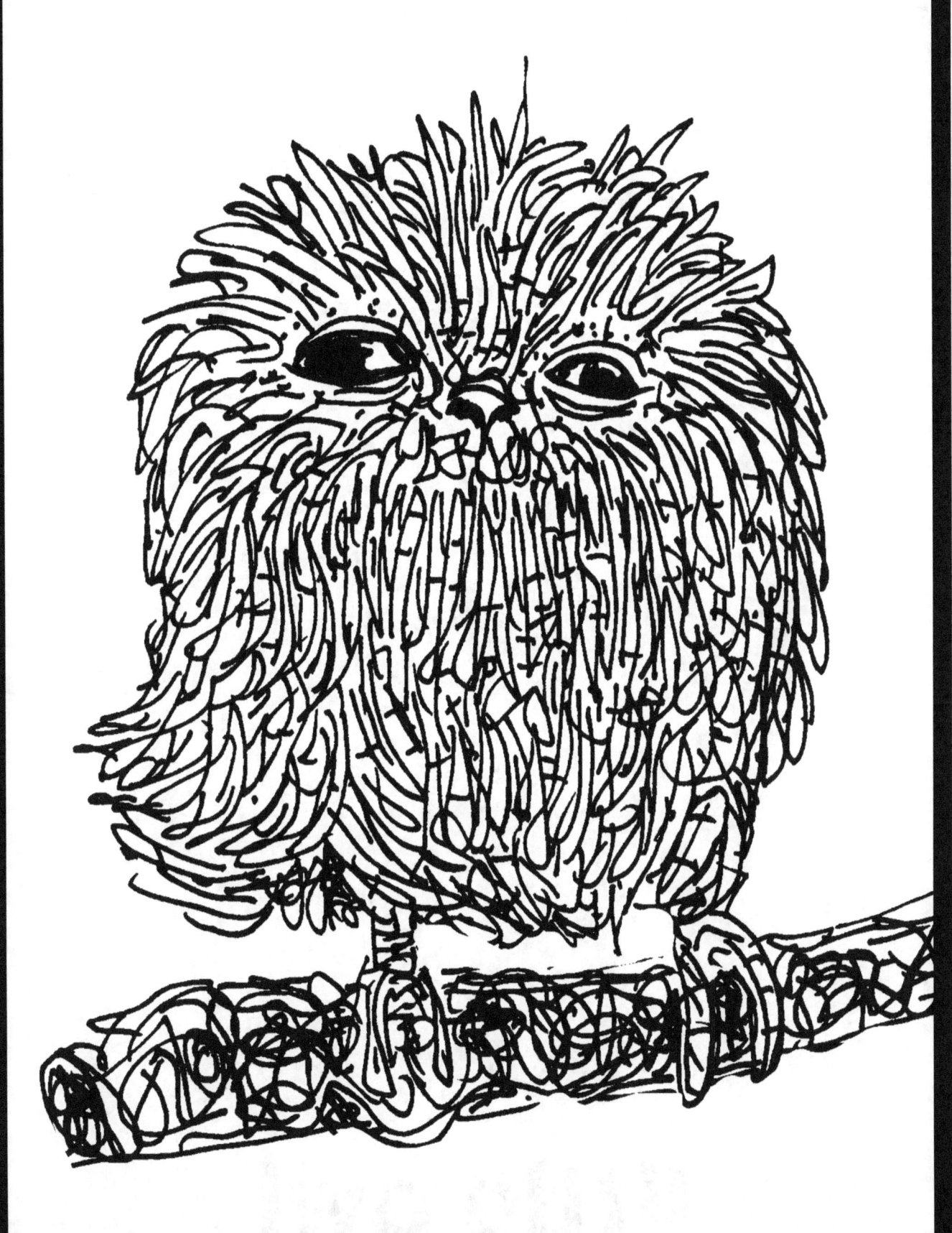

little owl

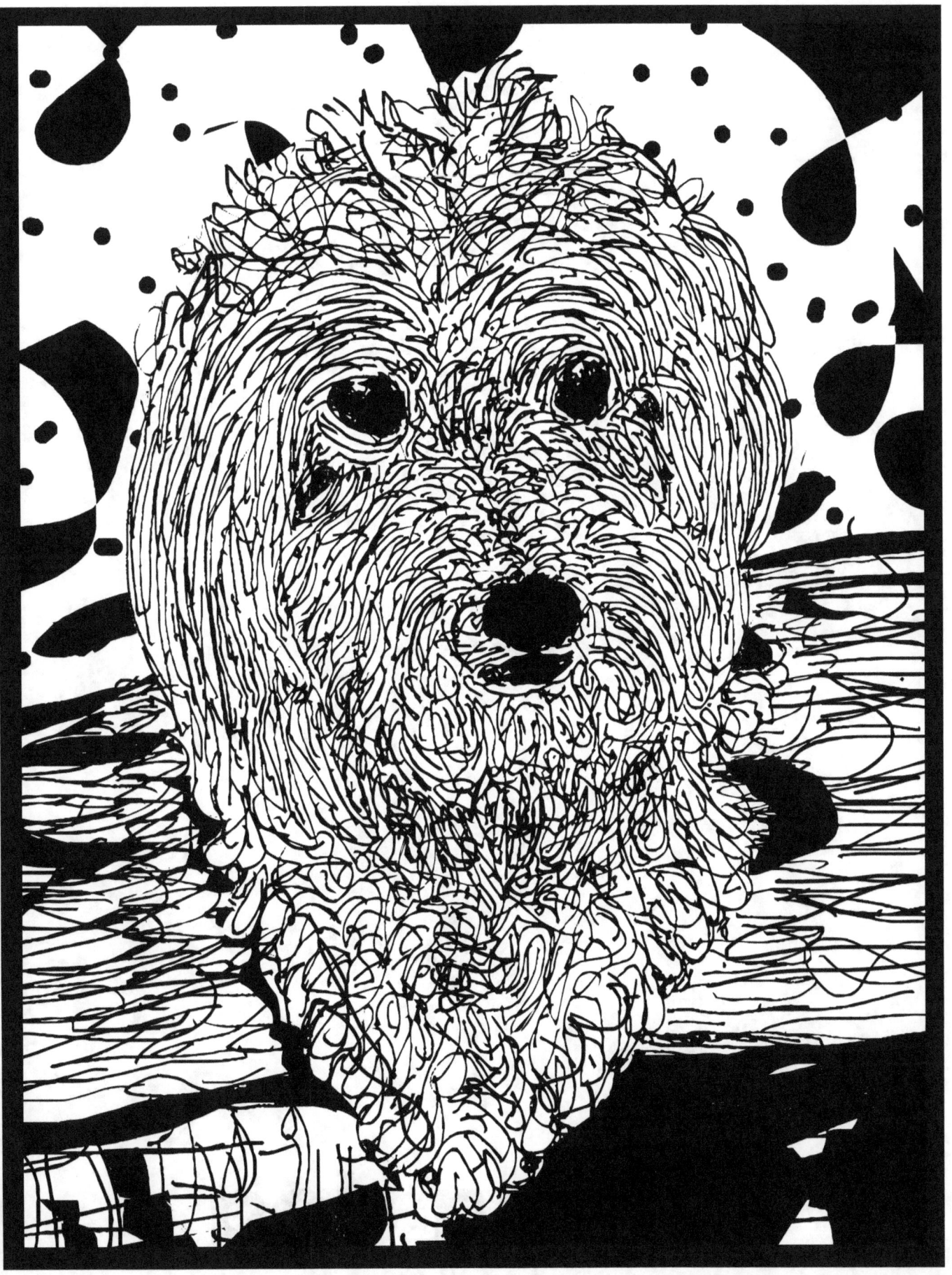

sitting dog

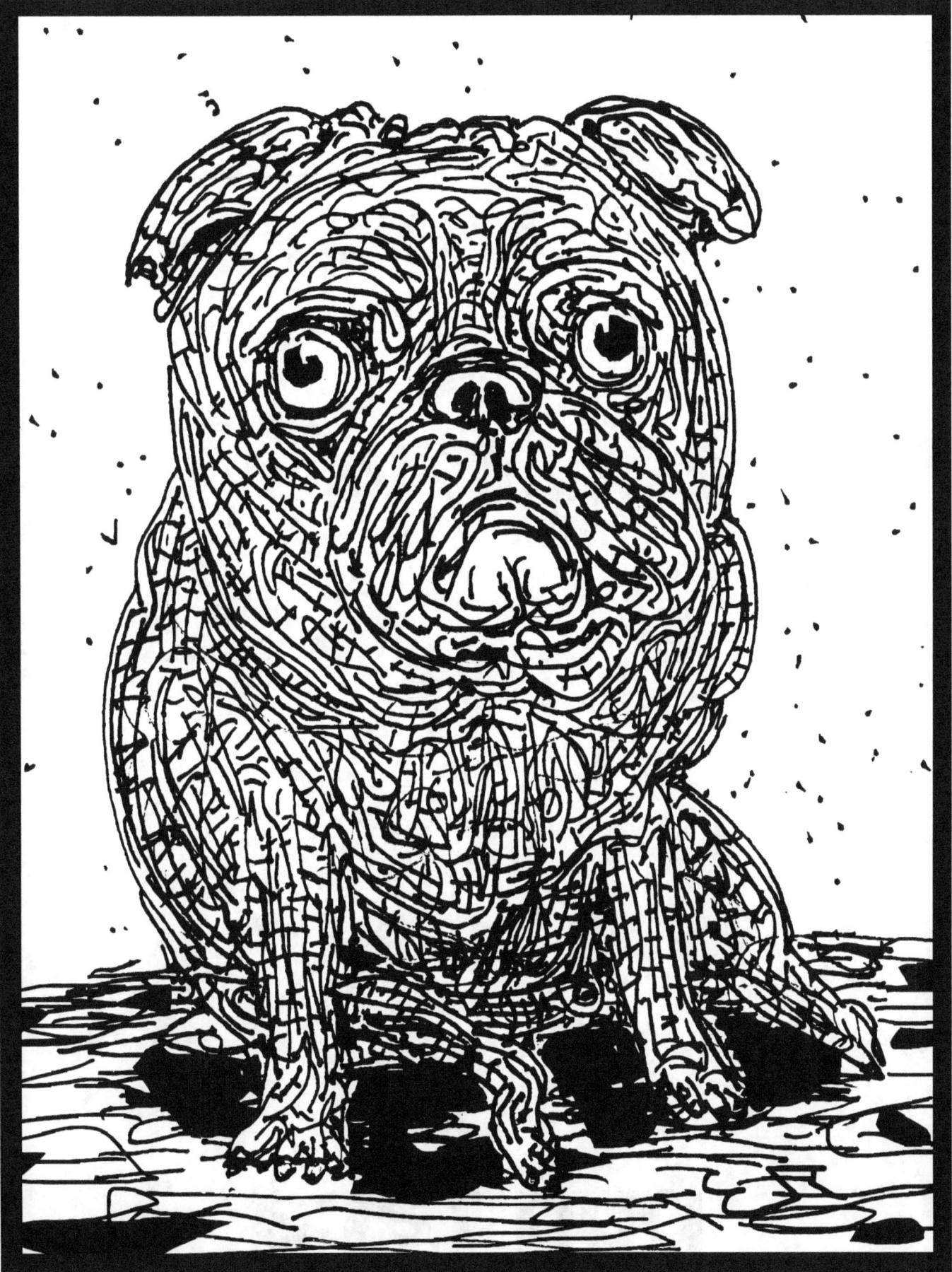

pug face

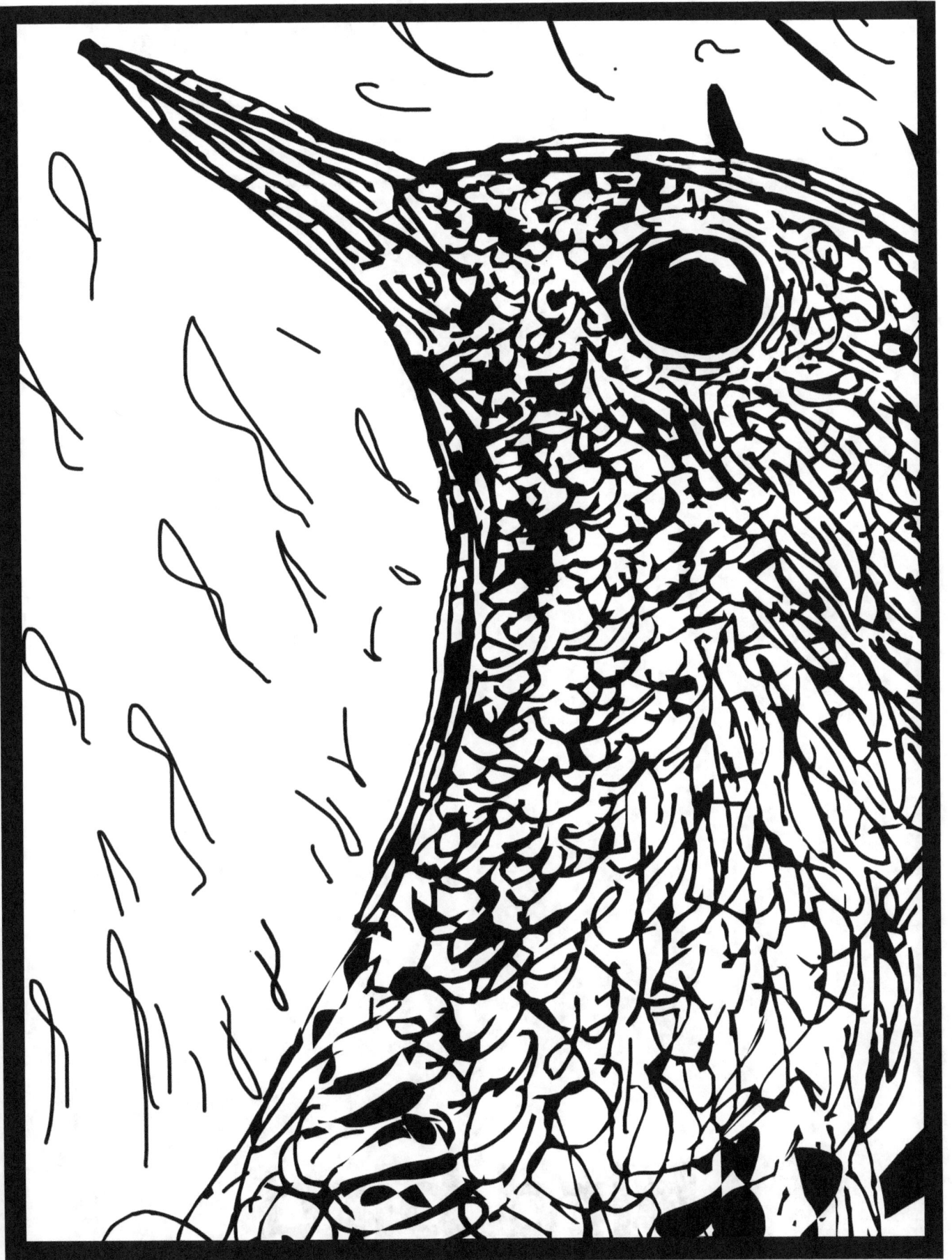

bird bird

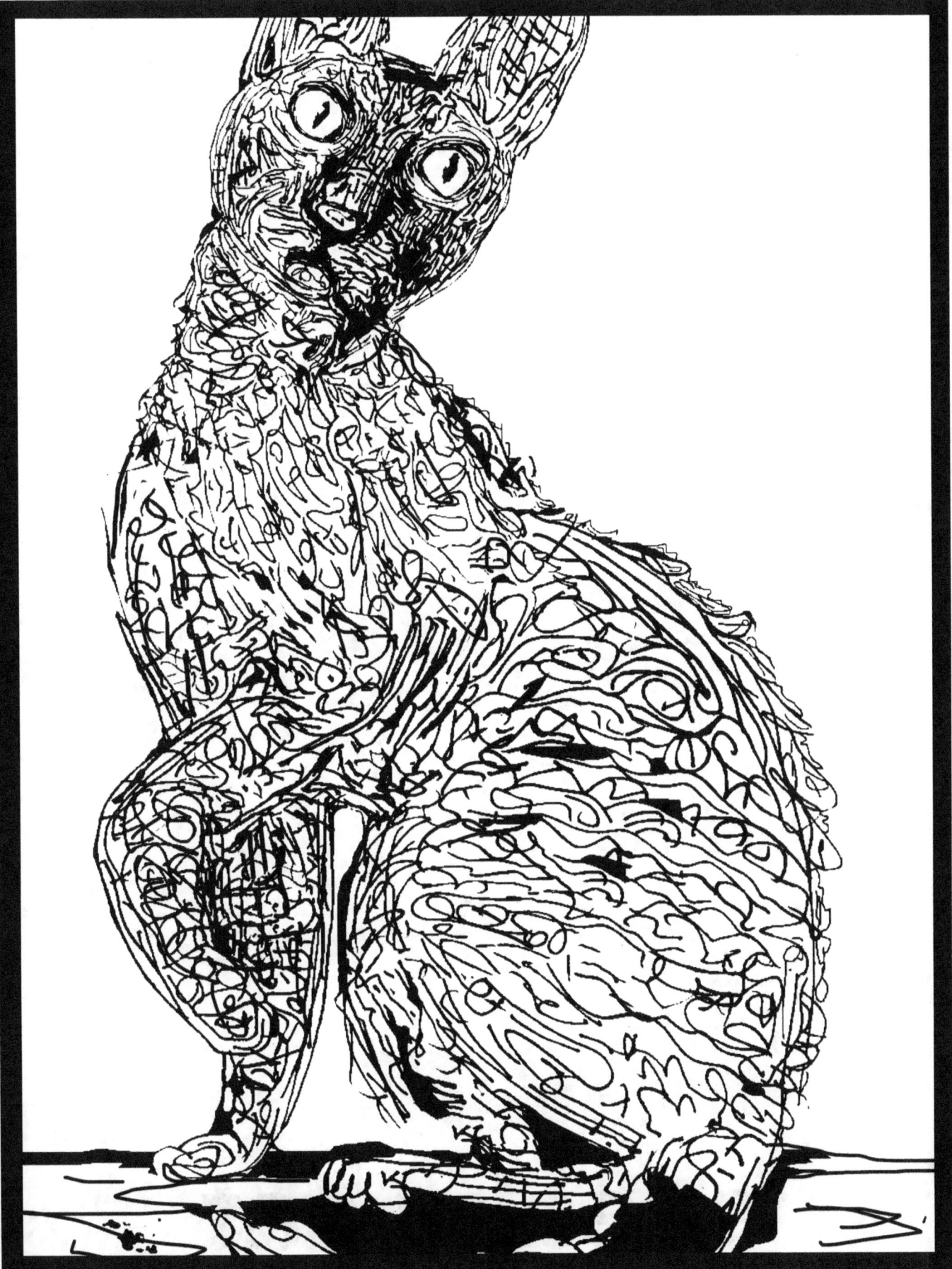

sneaky cat

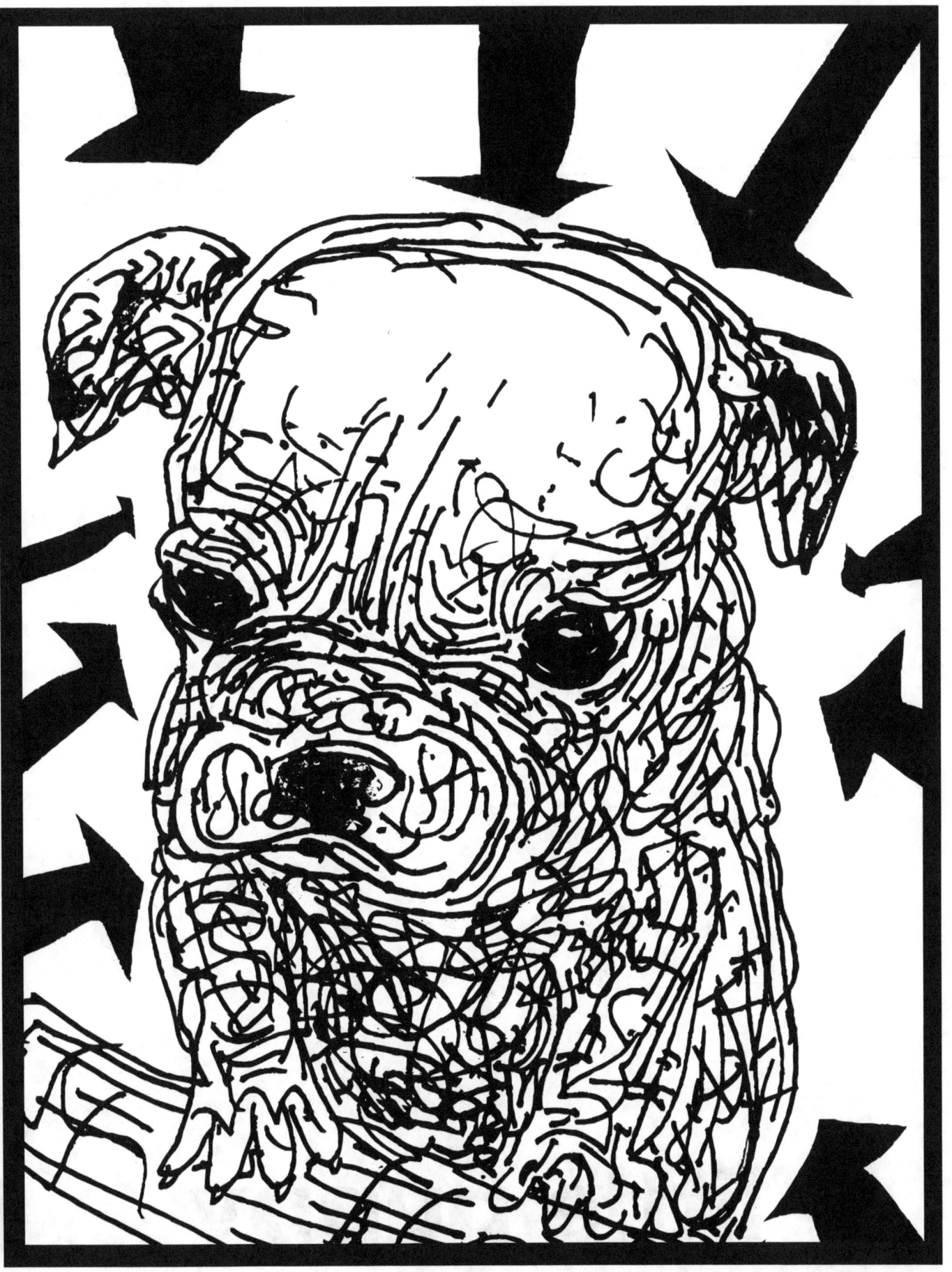

little puppy

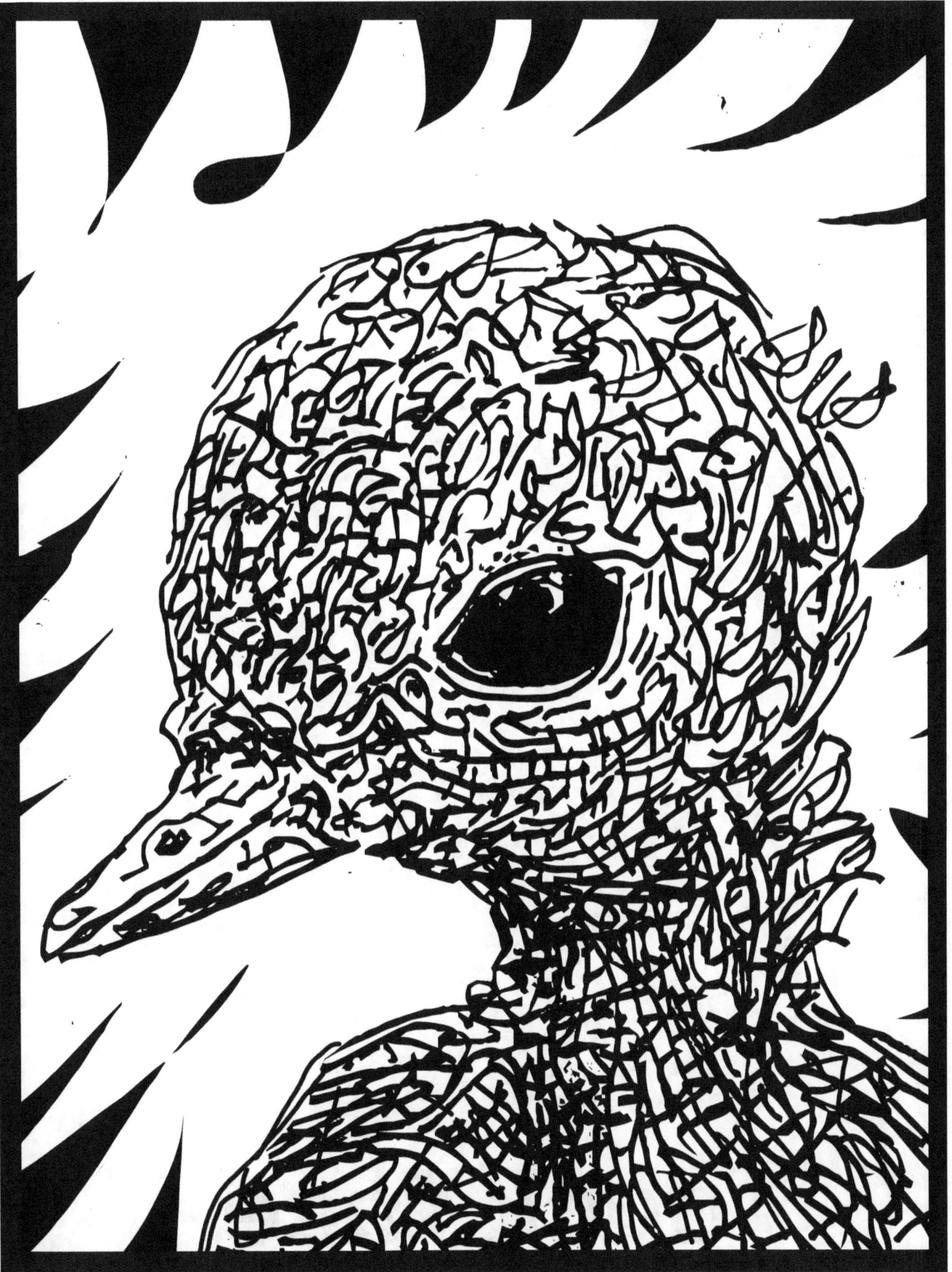

duck face

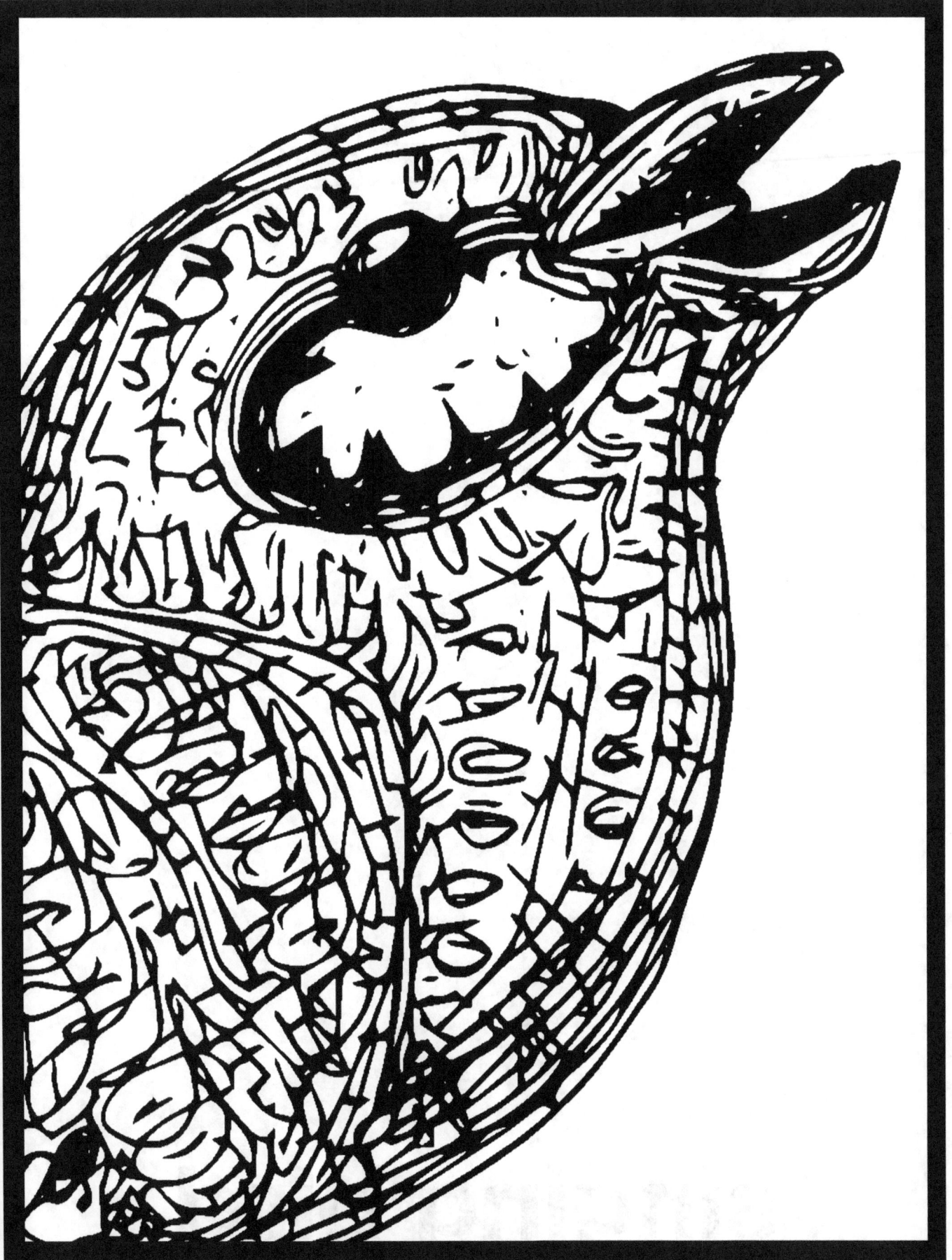

singing bird

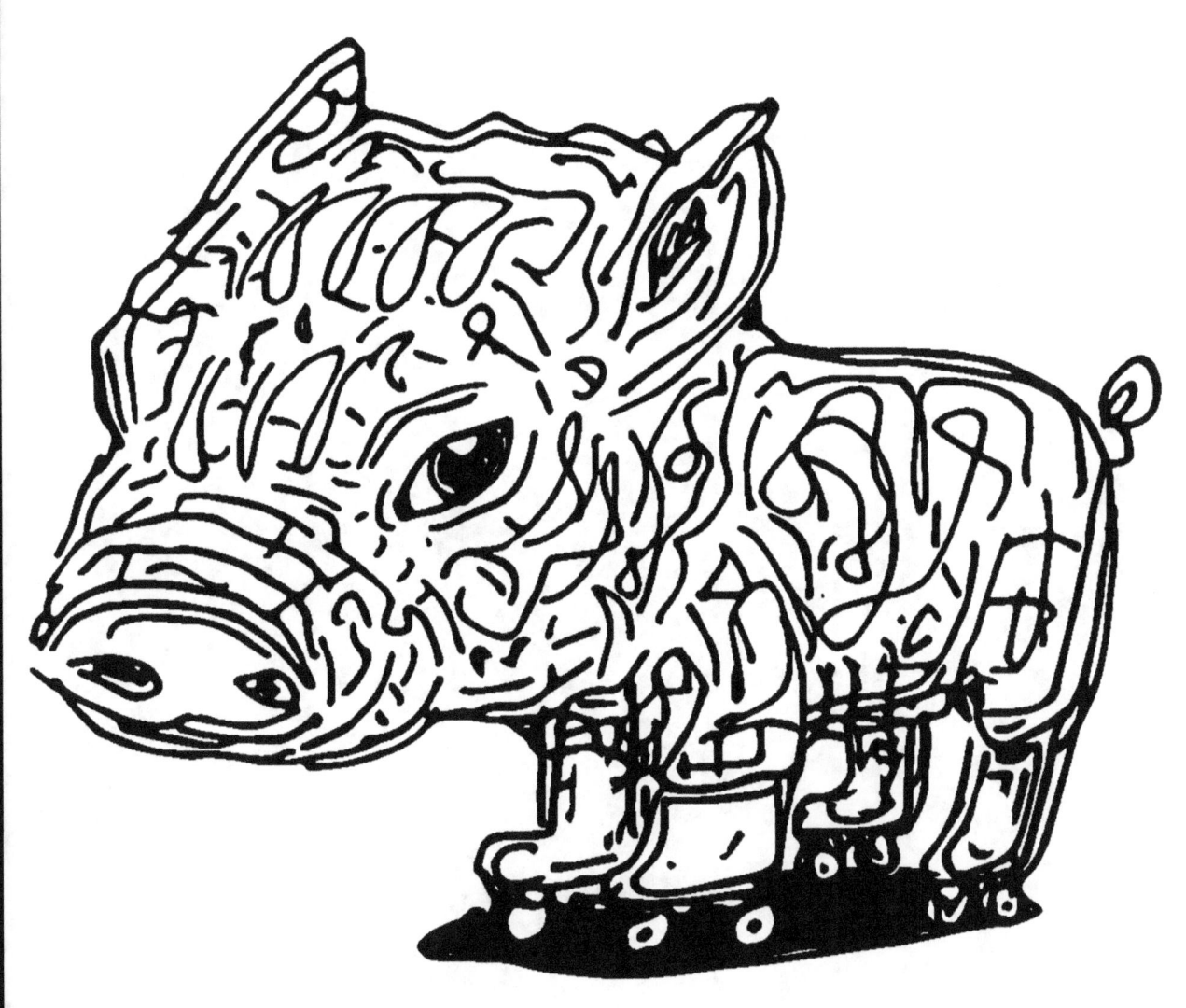

pig with skates

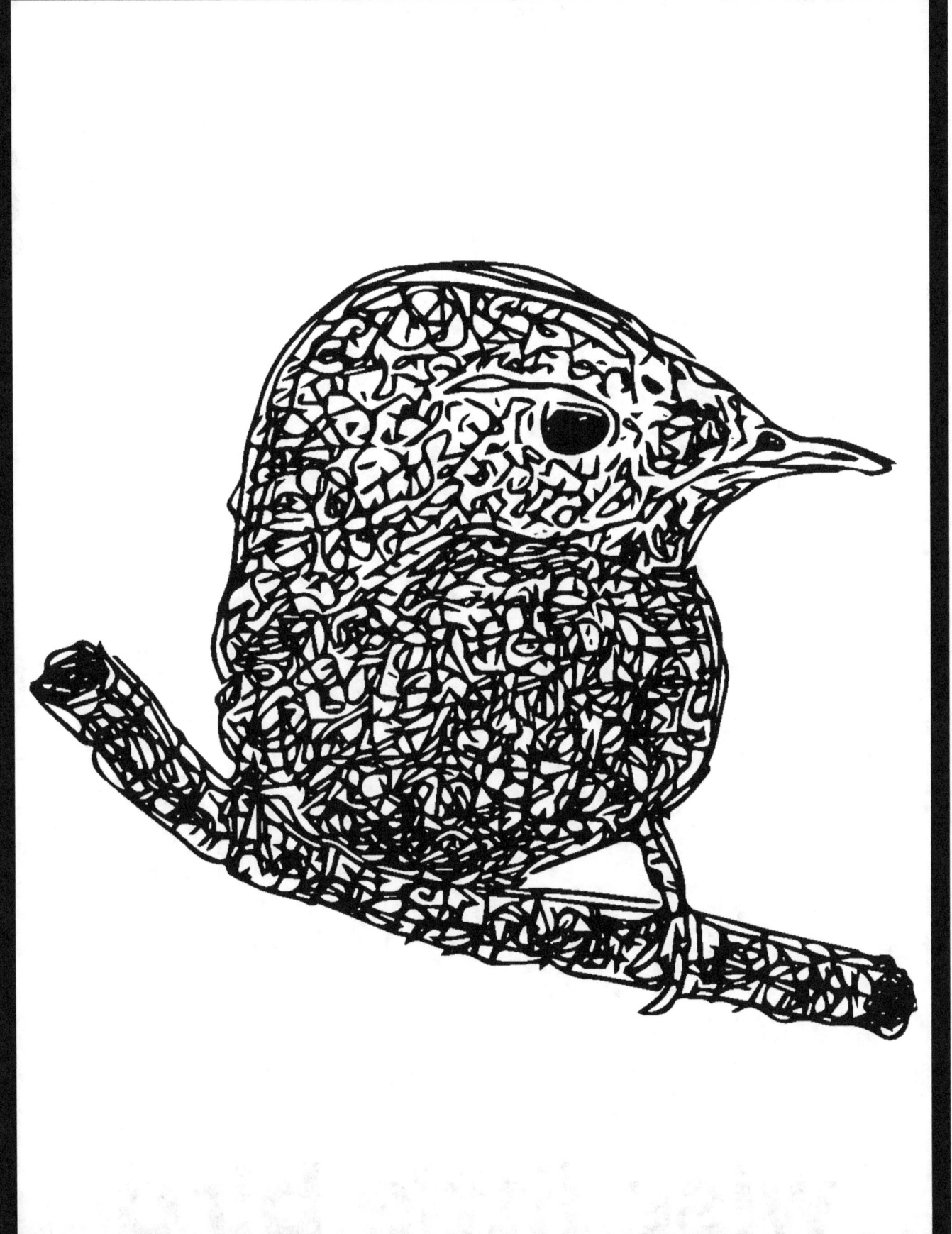

wise little bird

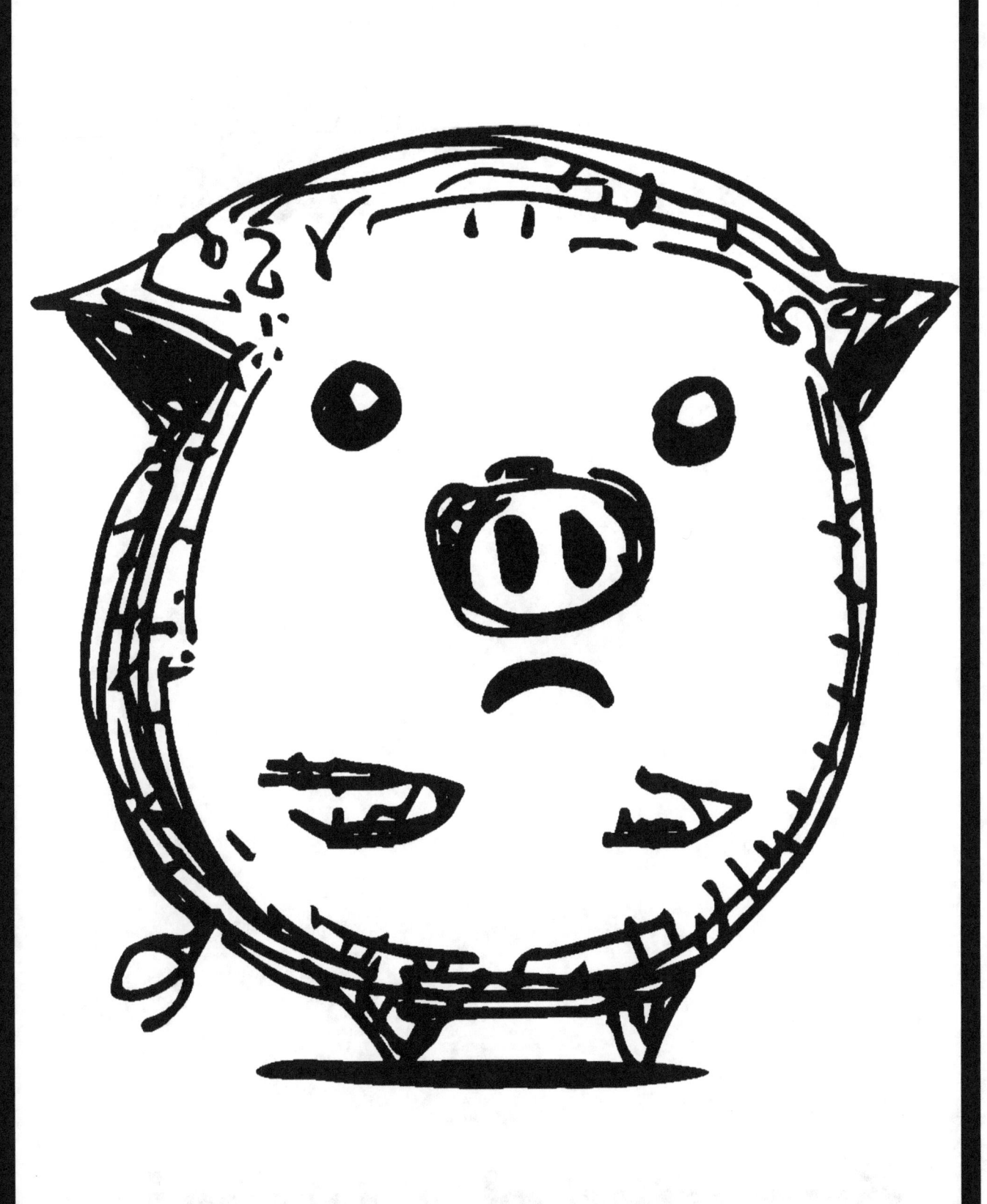

freaked out pig

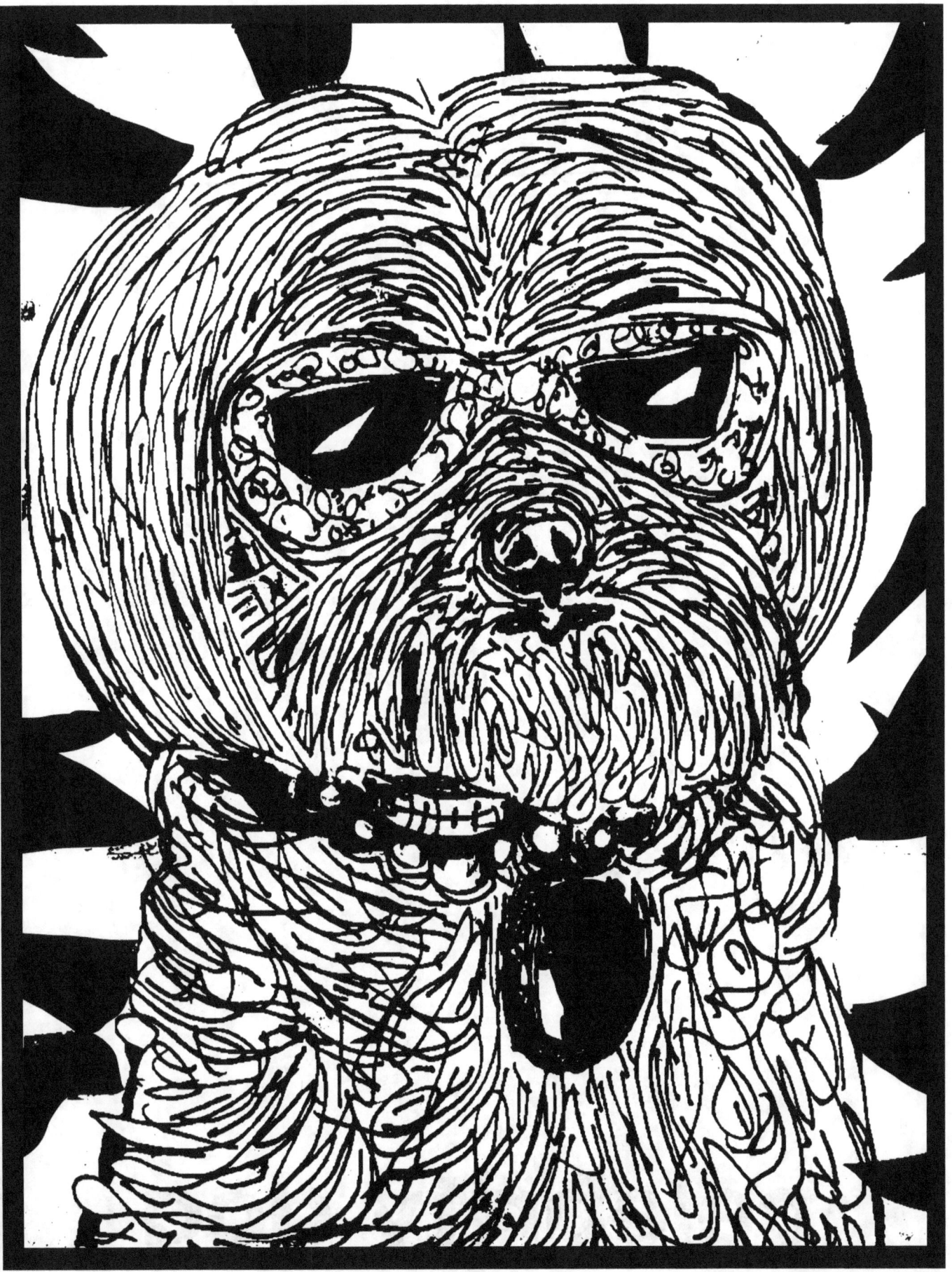

celebrity dog

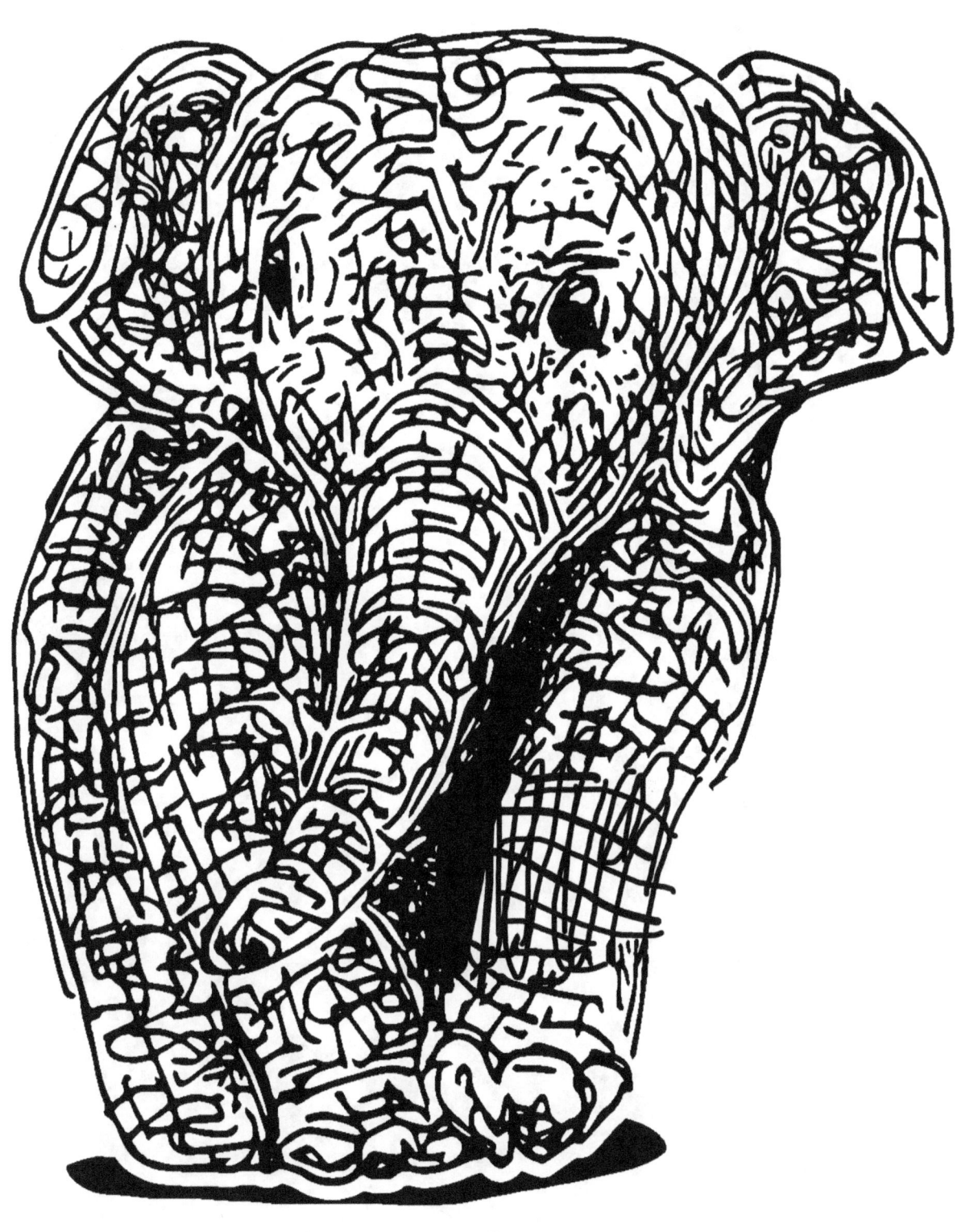

baby elephant

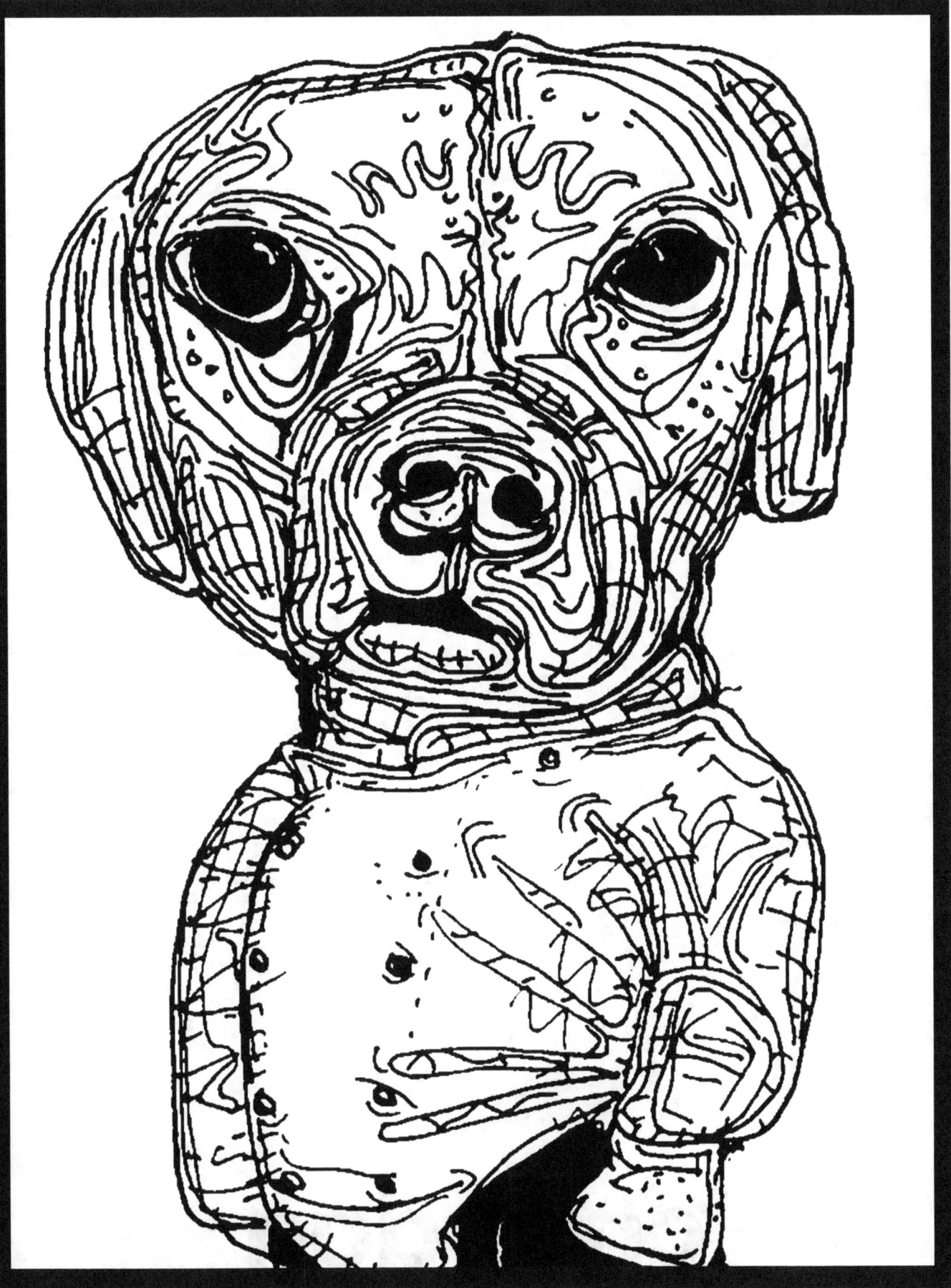

chef dog

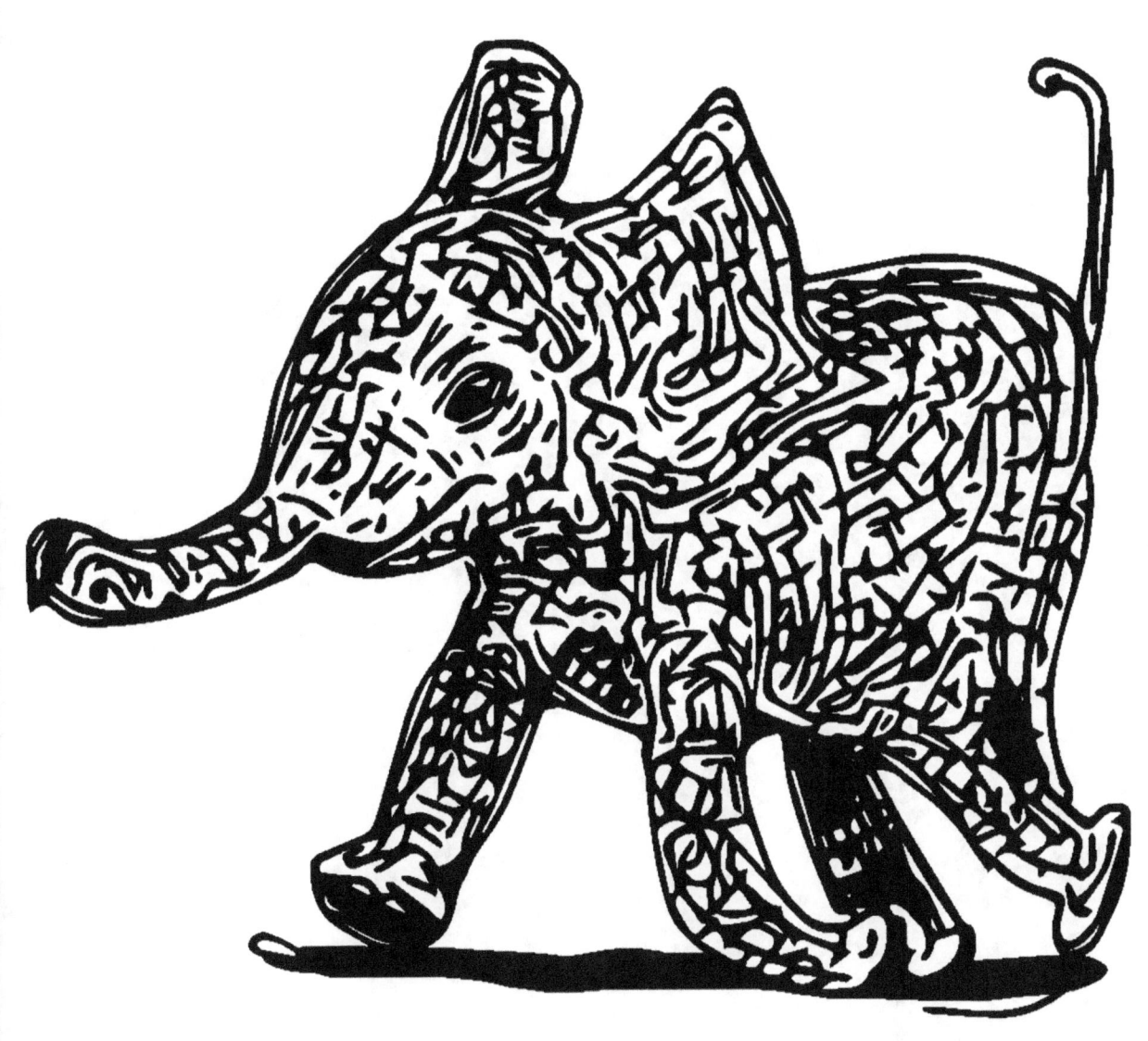

happy elephant

www.ingramcontent.com/pod-product-compliance
Lightning Source LLC
Chambersburg PA
CBHW080844170526
45158CB00009B/2622